WHAT'S FAIR

WHAT'S FAIR

Helping Us Cope with Life Issues

TYAWN A. MARTIN

authorHOUSE®

AuthorHouse™
1663 Liberty Drive
Bloomington, IN 47403
www.authorhouse.com
Phone: 1-800-839-8640

First published by AuthorHouse   07/20/2011

ISBN: 978-1-4634-3720-6 (sc)
ISBN: 978-1-4634-3719-0 (ebk)

Library of Congress Control Number: 2011912609

Printed in the United States of America

Any people depicted in stock imagery provided by Thinkstock are models, and such images are being used for illustrative purposes only.
Certain stock imagery © Thinkstock.

This book is printed on acid-free paper.

Because of the dynamic nature of the Internet, any web addresses or links contained in this book may have changed since publication and may no longer be valid. The views expressed in this work are solely those of the author and do not necessarily reflect the views of the publisher, and the publisher hereby disclaims any responsibility for them.

CHAPTER ONE

☛ A Way to Educate Trouble Teens ☚

Juveniles are all different no two are the same. But most of them start getting into trouble around their teenagers years. Between the ages of 13-18, is when they start to make all the wrong decisions. Which there are at the age to know what right and wrong? Some are influence younger ones to experience things they don't know about. They become rebellious and act out, start skipping school becomes boring. When their suspended for disruption or skipping classes, they use that as an excuse to hang out late at night. This when the change from young teens to juvenile delinquents. Juveniles tend to get bored with things at rapid pace, so when one things at rapid pace, so when one thing gets old they move or to next one. They began to experience the street life. They start experimenting with drugs, stealing from their families and friends. Depending on what type of influence a teen is under. They may even break into homes within their own community, then advancing to stores, cars and the list goes on. Drugs have different effects on teens but once they're experiences them their attitudes change. They're more disrespectful, rebellious towards their parents, siblings, teachers and anyone who has authority. I've also learned that all parents don't just give up on their kids. Some parents do go the extra mile to discipline. They talk back more.

It's even harder for a single mom to raise a young man then it is to raise a young woman. Which some moms has that control on their sons and some moms don't have that connection on should

I say bond with their sons. Every child is born with his or her own mine, so it's not always the parents. Once a teen experience the freedom to make their decisions that's when the trouble becomes easier to get into. Teens tend to commit more crimes because the punishment for their age range is what should be considered minimum punishment. Most trouble teen can't even read or spell but can cause harm to the kids who wants an education. When they reach that point of no return that's when the Juvenile Judicial System should step in and up the punishment. Some teens feel they want get much time or any time behind bars for some of the crime s their committing these days. Depending on the age shouldn't matter, especially when violent crimes are committed. Once a teen commits a crime and becomes incarcerated that should be a turning point in their lives. While incarcerated they should have school 12 hours a day, study 2 hours, recreational time 2 hours, 45 minutes apiece to eat breakfast, lunch, dinner and rest of the time sleep. T.V. a privilege and that should be earned. Phone calls and visits are considered privileges and freedom. My opinion it will in fact educate them, teach the importance of education, at the same time encourage them to go home and continue the effort to make something of themselves. The Judicial System now of days incarcerates young teens for long teens for long periods of time return them home the same as they left. Uneducated and ready to go find old friends who are on level as them who's up to no good or trouble! While incarnated they should have to maintain an A-B average, reading and studying are requirements. When you get a rebellious child that just don't want to learn push back or add more time to their sentencing, until they participate and understand education is the key out. Education is truly the key to being successful at something in life. The objective is to help them mentally, educationally, decrease violent crime amongst teens, lower drop outs rates, promotes healthy educated young and women. My opinion under this new rule where a child is not sentence to a certain length of time, but their freedom is up to them and their education. For parents who are going through problems with a young teen encourage them to go to school. Or encourage the Juvenile Judicial System to change and adopt this new way of punishment. I believe it would help parents, teachers specially and society. Also keep teens from running their lives at an early age. Change is an important word and Everyone Can!

Juveniles are all different no two are the same. But most of them start getting into trouble around their teenagers years. Between the ages of 13-18, is when they start to make all the wrong decisions. Which there are at the age to know what right and wrong? Some are influence younger ones to experience things they don't know about. They become rebellious and act out, start skipping school becomes boring. When their suspended for disruption or skipping classes, they use that as an excuse to hang out late at night. This when the change from young teens to juvenile delinquents. Juveniles tend to get bored with things at rapid pace, so when one things at rapid pace, so when one thing gets old they move or to next one. They began to experience the street life. They start experimenting with drugs, stealing from their families and friends. Depending on what type of influence a teen is under. They may even break into homes within their own community, then advancing to stores, cars and the list goes on. Drugs have different effects on teens but once they're experiences them their attitudes change. They're more disrespectful, rebellious towards their parents, siblings, teachers and anyone who has authority. I've also learned that all parents don't just give up on their kids. Some parents do go the extra mile to discipline. They talk back more.

It's even harder for a single mom to raise a young man then it is to raise a young woman. Which some moms has that control on their sons and some moms don't have that connection on should I say bond with their sons. Every child is born with his or her own mine, so it's not always the parents. Once a teen experience the freedom to make their decisions that's when the trouble becomes easier to get into. Teens tend to commit more crimes because the punishment for their age range is what should be considered minimum punishment. Most trouble teen can't even read or spell but can cause harm to the kids who wants an education. When they reach that point of no return that's when the Juvenile Judicial System should step in and up the punishment. Some teens feel they want get much time or any time behind bars for some of the crime s their committing these days. Depending on the age shouldn't matter, especially when violent crimes are committed. Once a teen commits a crime and becomes incarcerated that should be a turning point in their lives. While incarcerated they should have school 12 hours a day, study 2 hours, recreational time 2 hours, 45 minutes apiece to eat breakfast, lunch, dinner and rest of the time sleep. T.V. a privilege and that should be earned. Phone calls and visits are considered privileges and freedom. My opinion it will in fact educate them, teach the importance of education, at the same time encourage them to go home and continue the effort to make something of themselves. The Judicial System now of days incarcerates young teens for long teens for long periods of time return them home the same as they left. Uneducated and ready to go find old friends who are on level as them who's up to no good or trouble! While incarnated they should have to maintain an A-B average, reading and studying are requirements. When you get a rebellious child that just don't want to learn push back or add more time to their sentencing, until they participate and understand education is the key out. Education is truly the key to being successful at something in life. The objective is to help them mentally, educationally, decrease violent crime amongst teens, lower drop outs rates, promotes healthy educated young and women. My opinion under this new rule where a child is not sentence to a certain length of time, but their freedom is up to them and their education. For parents who are going through problems with a young teen encourage them to go to school. Or encourage the Juvenile Judicial System to change and adopt this new way of punishment. I believe it would help parents, teachers specially and society. Also keep teens from running their lives at an early age. Change is an important word and Everyone Can!

CHAPTER TWO

How to Punish
Those Who Commit Crimes

For the last couple years we have heard about the crime rate growing. People are being killed by a gunshot or drunk driver. My question is why and how does guns and alcohol end up in the wrong's person hand. How can the jurisdictions system punish those who commit harsh crimes, such as murder, robberies, rape, and even the child molester? They should have laws that would send those people to fight in the war we are having in America without pay. I feel the government spends more money feeding certain criminals for free, when the money can be used to feed those families who lost their homes do to a natural cause. Prison is a camp to some of the inmates. Some don't even spend 90 days in jail. Today guns are the biggest problem of children deaths. How many kids or people have to die before the government, President realizes they have to step up their plans on stopping gun violence. It shouldn't be easy for anyone to be able to purchase a weapon such as a gun. There should be only one gun shop in every state. Only an officer of the law should issue these dangerous weapons. The price for gun should be a better way to punish those people who uses a gone to take another person life. They who kill would have two choices. One would be to sacrifice our own life, second would be the death chair. Why give them a second chance to take another person life rather their home on in jail? Taken someone from their families by killing them is a sad and scary thing. Put all of the people that commit murder in the jungle overseas and let them run free with all the wild animals. Now they would have to survive on their own. The punishment might sound harsh but it teaches a person how important another human is to them. We need each other in this world and someone who kills need to be taught a lesson. I feel putting them in the jungle world save the government money because the system want have to feed, or cloths them. The world hearing about this new law would change and drop the murder crime rate dramatically. I believe that. That goes for men and women. Even now you hear more and more about parents taking their kids' lives. When did all this started and why do these tragic moments happen? If only the government would step in and past the law where guns can't be sold on the streets or at guns shows without license. There will be less kids or teens with guns in their possession. The crime rate of kids being killed by another youth would drop a lot. Think about the families who lost a love one or child to gun violence. The guns that are made today should only up to 5 rounds. Just think it would work. I agree that knifes can be conceder a weapon. How many people you know that have been killed by a person driving a car throwing knife and drive a car at the same time. I know it's easy to drive and shoot a gun. We all have heard of a drive by. A person has a better chance getting away from a knife then a gun. You know the distance of a bullet and a knife coming at you. You also will have better chance of living from a stab wound.

Now guys who commit crimes such as criminal's domestic violence should be sent to the army to fight in the war, without pay. Any man who hit woman should be able to fight for their country without pay. Men before you hit that woman, think about how you got here on earth. Now than any woman for the pain they went thru, before and after having a baby. No man can do that. I know that's true! For all men who have woman problems, walk away. Please it works, I know. I have done it.

Now open your mind about Child Molesters. Why are these people only getting a light sentence when punish buy the law. Those who commit such type of crime are people we all trust not to do such thing. Stop and think, now imagine how a person touching a child private part can their way of thinking. Just that one time can corrupt a child mind. Some kids don't even know what's being done to them. To me that's a sad thing to hear or see a helpless child going thru that. This is a reason why a lot of young girls act as if it their already grown because an older person touches her at a young age. It's hard to believe the people who you think are committing this type crime. Preachers, teachers, relatives, and coaches are some of the ones we wouldn't believe that are doing this to the kids.

That's why I feel child molester punishment should be cruel and harsh. Those are some of the people we could blame for a lot of teen pregnancy today. Let's help the government change the law so that we can keep these sex predators away from our kids. All we have to do is voice our opinion.

What about the people commit crimes such as robberies? How many you done been robbing before? How would you feel coming home to a broke in home knowing you didn't leave it that way? I know it hurts to come home and see your home done being demolish. All the items you have work for someone have took them. It can be a relative or friend of yours. There are so many corner stores and bank robberies going on around you today that just have to stop. It's time to put a stop to this. We all have families that work in these places. If the punishment or jail time was 15 years to life max. Make sure they who commit robberies do their whole sentence incarcerated. No early release at all under any circumstances. I promise there would be fewer robberies. It's a scarier thing to go thru, when someone pointing a gun at you demanding your money or personal belongings.

CHAPTER THREE

How to Help the Mothers and Fathers Cope With the Responsibility of Raising a Child?

This chapter is for all ages of parents, teens, and elders. First thing as parents we have to understand that it's not the child who asked to be here. Parents never speak as if it was the child fault when your life changes for the one a baby. It's both the male and female responsibility. But if both partners was to sit down before having this child they would both have the understanding of the other person feels about having kids at this time in their life. In a relationship it's mainly the woman's idea to start a family. Men are more willing to have a child to please his girlfriend/spouse. Most men aren't really ready to have children because they fell as if they are still young and not really stable in their lives.

As a teenage boy/young adult you might think the idea of a child is good because of feel like you're in love but that child comes greater with responsibility. And as a teenager you haven't grown up yourself talking about raising a baby. It's already hard on a man when he learns that he will be a father. The first thing he does is stress about money and how much he has. The biggest fear is wondering if you will have enough to support this child plus you and your spouse. For the teenage fathers that don't have jobs to support their child/children leave the responsibility on their parents. Just because you know your parents will always be there for you it's not their responsibility to your job, but as parents they know how hard the struggle will be so they take this child as their own. Now the father is placed on what the world called child support.

The child support system is considered a law to make a parent of the child pay money to the guardian who had custody of the baby. The odds in this world are more fathers then mothers on child support. Some women put men on child support because mother and father of the child have separated. But that don't mean the father doesn't care for his children. Some women use child support system to their advantage to hurt the father of their child financially. They seem to know the child support system will have him going to court so that a judge can order him to pay the mother of the child money once a week or month. Now that's not counting the money the father has the child with him. There are mothers who choose to ask for more money because they feel they deserve more.

Now the more money the father makes the more he have to pay. Is that fair to the fathers, who is getting the money? The child can't cash checks or spend the money. What if the father makes a million dollars a year and is order to twenty five thousand dollars a month. Is that much money necessary? Do you really think a two year old baby needs that much money a month? That money benefits the mother or guardian of the child more then it will benefit the child. As a mother in this situation you should try harder to achieve more for you and your child. Putting the father of your child on child support will get you the benefits you might need but now let's stop and think who it benefit more. What about the fathers who does more for his then the mother does? Should he have to pay child support, when you have some fathers out here who are not taking care of their responsibilities? Sure they should be punished for leaving behind their responsibility and also having leaving her to raise a baby on her own. Don't forget about the fathers who are raising their children on their children on their own! Give him the same treatment. Most dads will try to handle the issue without putting the mother of their child on child support. Some men prides are high so they don't ask for help or government assistance. If there was another method or medicine for men to take besides condoms there will be less unplanned pregnancies. Even less fathers on child support. Believe it or not there are plenty men out here in this world that would use every method possible they are not ready to have kids. If only there was a doctor or scientist who could invent a drug that could slow down the male sperm count. Just think about how many kids living in a one parent home because the father wasn't ready to be a father. I do believe that this invention would help not only males but females who could be allergy to condoms.

Think about how many ways a woman can prevent having a baby. There are at least five methods that they can take or use. To all the men who are on child support please pay even when you know in your heart that you do for your child. Don't let anger you have for the child support system between the loves you have for your kids. Farther please understand that when you enter a child's life they look up to you. Here's away: take out sometime and talk to the mother of the child. Ask how much money would be reasonable a week or once a month. "That's what I did" believe me it help me for eleven years so far. My oldest son is eleven and I love him so much. Giving money to his mother would not stop what I do for him. Once again fathers keep up the good work.

CHAPTER FOUR

How Can You Tell If His A Good Man

Not every man is a bad man but as a woman you have to know what you want in order to find a good man. But for the ones who feel like they have tried and did everything to find a good man here are something's you may have skipped.

Before you put a label on him get to know him first. Start by wanting to be his friend and learn everything you can before rushing a relationship. If you are a woman with kids see how he acts towards your children because that is the most important thing. See what his life is heading; make sure he has goals for his future. Make sure he is always treating you with respect. Remember if he doesn't respect mother he want respect you!!! Try to be more than just lovers. Look for someone who can be your best friend, make sure he someone who can bring sunshine to your raining day.

Don't ever think that a good man can't do wrong because every man makes mistakes nobody is perfect. But don't let that stop you from patching up any broken pieces. As a woman when we do find what we feel is a good man we have to cherish him and show him how much we really care. A good man wants to be treated like you would want him to treat you. Show him that you appreciate him and that the love will always be there no matter what storm brings. We always hear people say man never cherish what they have till it's gone. Well ladies that statement goes for us as well. In this generation today it's harder to find a good man because we are so blinded by what we think is something when it's nothing. There is someone for everyone and will treat you like you want to be treated. Just do your best not to mess it up always let your relationship build off love? Leaving you with something to think about, you will never know what a good man looks like because looks tell you nothing about a person. So don't judge them by the way they may look or the color of their skin because beauty is skin deep. But remember just because he is a good man doesn't mean his good for you!!!

Someone　　　　　　　*Respect*
Understanding　　　　*Equal*
Caring　　　　　　　*Lenient*
Compromise　　　　　*Assure*
Erotic　　　　　　　*Talk*
Strong　　　　　　　*Impassioned*
Stoical　　　　　　　*Observe*
Faithful　　　　　　*Nourish*
Unconditional　　　　*Sharing*
Love　　　　　　　　*Honesty*
　　　　　　　　　　Inseparable
　　　　　　　　　　Persistence

Too Good to Be True

I'm here even when you can't see

Just a breath away when you in need

Unconditional love without a fee

A good man is what you call me

Being who I am is not easy

My love for you is strong like a tree

Now I hear you speak as in we

Questions you ask I can't answer please

Ready I'm not nor should I be

In my eyes you are a queen

Hurting you mentally I won't conceive

I car to much so I leave

CHAPTER FIVE

 **Teenage Pregnancy**

To all the young teenage women who don't have kids. Please take a look at some of the women who have children and what they're going through. You only get one chance at life so take your time and do what's best for you. Having a baby can be a wonderful thing even better if you are stable. For all the women that want to have kids. Please think about your future first. Keep in mind that everything takes time in life. No need to rush things. Ask yourself, what do you want to be life? Try to accomplish your dreams of dream first. Think on how you can better yourself financially. I know as a young woman or teenager, you wonder can you produce kids. Ladies let nature take its place when the time is right for you. Get all you can get out of life as a young woman before becoming a mother. It's harder on teenage mom then someone who waited later in their life to have kids. A child can take up all your time. Some kids need extra attention. I know some you teenage girls see your friend with a baby and think it's cute. Some even think having a baby makes them grown but it doesn't. There are women who have kids so that they can receive government assistance. There are woman that feels that way. Sure the Government helps the mothers with assistance for them and the child! The mothers receive stamps which pay for food tax free. They offer health insurance. With the government giving all this free help to the new moms or mothers who are still having kids. The help makes some of the mothers lazy. Plenty of them give up on life, live off assistance they receive from the government. Young women or mothers and older ones. Especially single mothers help them! We all know it's hard out here in this world. That's why as parents we should teach our kids the truth about life. You have some parents who accept their child having a baby early in life. For example you might hear a parent talk as if their happy to be a grandparent. But what about your child future, are she ready to take on the responsibility of raising a child. Every parent knows their child, so we should if their ready to take that big step in life. Mother let your daughter know the outcome of being a single parent and it's not easy.

CHAPTER SIX

 **Is Life Fair to Everyone**

My opinion would be no. Because you have people that goes military and fight in the war for their country. Those same people risk their lives for less money than someone who works at a restaurant. Not only the pay is bad but what about the years they spend away from their family. Some return home with health issues. Then you have those who don't return home at all. Why does a person who fights for our country have to be marry for his or her kids to receive the health benefit that their parents lost their for. Think on how the family feels after losing a love one. Do you think the pay is worth a child fearing that they would never see their mom or dad again? Think about what a soldier go through and see while he or she overseas. Some of them see death in their face up close every day. Now you tell me is their pay fair. Would you sacrifice your life for your country at the pay role it's. Why do teachers get paid less than lawyers, doctors, judges? When a teacher should get paid the same as a person they have taught to become a successful doctor. Think about the time spent teaching a child how to read, write just their own names. That's just the start. Let's not forget about the spelling. This one teacher has taught a class of 20 to 30 kids an hour at a time for 8 hours a day. Now add up how many kids that day. Think about how many attitudes from each child a teacher has to put up with a day. What about the ones who don't want to learn? That teacher still has to try hard to teach those individuals. For the last couple years we have been asking why our teachers give up on their jobs as teachers. You may hear many teachers say they don't get paid enough. This is true.

I feel the government needs to stop and realize that it's our teachers who are teaching their children to learn about life. Maybe if the school district was able to pay these teachers what they deserve they would put forward effort. There's teachers who put their all and heart into teaching. Even into those kids that needs the extra attention. What about the teachers who work overtime to help a certain student. Teachers have families at home that they have to deal with after leaving a job dealing with other people kids. You have famous people, doctors, lawyers, celebrity that can afford to pay someone to watch their kids. But a teacher has to go home and deal with their own family issues. Do you think a teacher pay is fair. I feel they should get paid a lot more than what their salary are today. Maybe if the pay goes up there would be more teachers that care. You would have more kids wanting to become teachers when they grow up and finish school. Everyone has to go to school. So ask yourself how much you learned from a teacher so think the teacher. Everyone learns from a teacher so thank the teacher we have today for what they're taught the people in this world today. You have teacher who still owe student loans. Some have to work 2 and 3 years to pay off their student loans. Teachers should enter school every day with a smile not because of their pay. Smile because they're about to change a student life with some new knowledge. This means there is a better chance of more children getting a high school diploma.

CHAPTER SEVEN

 **Education Today**

Every day we hear about the education lottery but how much of the money is spent on the schools. We have over a hundred schools and not enough money to support the needs of them. Some schools can't afford to give out books because there population is so big. Every year schools are getting more and more students but not enough space in the classrooms. It's hard for children to get a descent education when the schools district can't afford the materials they need. I feel the government has forgotten about how hard it is for some public schools. For example if you were to go to a private school where there are rich students with rich parents. They seem to get a better education. Now step down to our lower class family who kids have to attend public schools with about 30 to 32 students packed in one classroom. They probably share books because the teachers don't have many to pass around.

Education is a major factor in this world so every child should get the same amount of education. It shouldn't matter what kind of school your child go to. Most people can't afford to send their child to a private school because of the price. Just sending your child to Daycare might cost you a hundred dollars to the least for one child that's about 2 month. It's not fair to those families who can't afford to pay 3000 dollars a semester. Every single child deserves to get the same education as the next child. Yes most folks may want their children in a private school but when you see the cost it's not affordable for everyone. Education is very important these days so we as America should push harder for a better education system to be able to support the young kids who are growing up today. And let's stop putting house payments on these kids just so they can graduate.

What I mean is why children are paying so much just to walk across the stage. College is so hard now days because you have to pay more than you can afford every semester just to stay in school. The most sad thing is you pay all this money and still don't have a chance or get the job you went to school for. Why can't education be free for the kids who want to learn? Even the ones who graduate spend 3 years or more paying back student loans. Some of the students graduate over qualify for the job they went to college for. Is that fair to someone who looks forward to the job title they chose. If the lottery is label Education Lottery then must of the money should be used towards the schools. So that kids want have to pay so much for education. Let's work together to keep the children in school and of the streets. Education is what we all need to be successful.

CHAPTER EIGHT

 **Poor, Race, Money**

Helping the less fortunate to overcome the issue of being poor. Poor is someone who has no money or a place to call home. How does someone become poor and homeless? Every poor person has their reason for being poor or how they became poor. Some people have less education and no help from anyone to get them back on track. There are smart homeless people on this earth. So education is not always the issue for a poor homeless person. You have people who lost everything they had to do to a natural cost. There also people who have done bad things to others and now they can't get the help they need in life do to their bad ways or habits. I feel the people who do have a little extra give to the needed. Could the world in all the poorness that goes on around us every day? My opinion would be no. My "fact" is that you or us as the people in the world can change some poor personal life to the point where they can help themselves.

A rich person can become poor. So being poor can happen to anybody. To avoid bring in that situation you have to know how to spend and manage your money. Someone who is or consider their self's to be poor would do just about anything to get money, cloths, or food. You have people who commit crimes such as murder, robberies, shoplifting just for a better living but it's not fair to the people who work hard for a better living for their families. It's hard to live in America as poor person because everything cost money.

Today the recession hurts the poor more than the rich. My reason for saying that is because if you don't have money now you would have a hard time finding a job to get way.

What about the victims of a natural cause that lost everything. Some of them lost their families, jobs, homes. To me that's the meaning of poor. Just think how you can go to sleep one night with everything you love and work hard for. Then awake with nothing. Now that's a hurting feeling. Think about New Orleans, Haiti. Look at how the Haitians are suffering without the money or help they need to save their own lives plus others. In my eyes that's living in fear every day. You have families who can't find their love ones or kids. Just turn on your T.V. and see all the people who still need our help. Remember poorness don't come with a choice. So let's get a system going to help these people who needed the most. Why adopt a child just for a credit write off or a charity case and tax write off. Don't just help a child help a family. Let's start helping more and less judging. Give jobs to those who need work in the United States. By sending them who want to work over to countries that need homes built for the people who lost their homes do to a natural cause.

It's not just the government job or president who has to help with an issue due to the poorness that goes on around us. If you are helping and sending money thank you I appreciate what you done. Don't put the pressure or responsibility on one person. We as Americans see and know about the poorness going on around us but it's not your fault. But you can help change what you see. The people in the world shouldn't look for a celebrity to always be the one who seen money to help those who are victims of a natural disasters. Why put so much spot light on a person who is famous. How about use the money from the lottery to build homes for the less fortunate. There are millions of dollars spent on fancy cars and cloths but there are people who can't even afford either one.

What can make all different race of people get alone? Money is so powerful that it can bring together enemies. Just look at a movie and see the race in all the actors in that one movie. In the movie you would see two of the different race of people kissing, sexing, and etc. Now if they were just regular low class people. You probably want see all that going on without other people looking as if that's a problem. Money can bring happiness and issues to all of us. One thing I can tell you that are true. You are going to need money to survive in this world today, tomorrow and in the future. The day that we want need money to live would be the day that electricity would be free. Can you imagine no light bills or gas bill? Three things that cost money, you would have to have. Baths, cloths, food. A green sheet of paper rules the world. Money is so powerful it can change your whole life for the best or worst. It can bring you together for the love of wanting it or to keep it. Think about how the Mexicans go through whatever it takes to get to the United States. To get money for a better living.

Its money considers being recent? Sure because if you don't have any you would be treated different. A person who is homeless would be treated different from someone who drives a Bentley.

Why pay Mexicans less money than an American. They work and do just the same as a person who are an Untied States Citizens. It's the people who have less money investing in those who have more than them. Look at how some Mexicans live would you want to live like that. I can understand their reason for trying to get to America. Have you ever thought about how American money means more in other countries such as Mexico?

Why does Racism still exist and when will it end. Racism is a big issue that has being going on for years. But we all try to teach the kids that are born in this world today that color doesn't matter. But when the young ones grow up and run into that problem what you can tell them now. What about the kids that has parents from different race. So how should that child be treated and what side should it takes. When that child will love their parents the same way no matter what color or language they speak. Think on and about the fear that child will face growing up in this world full of racism. People judging you on your color more than your education and smartness. You tell me is that fair for a child who has no control on how his or her parents met. It's not their ideal to have parents who are different race. To me "no child should have to face that problem or be treated different. Just about anything you do or get involve with might have a racist issue?

Just a simple conversation can in up on a racism subject. Try to talk about politics between to different race and see how far it goes. See if you can avoid feeling racist. You cannot even go out in public with two different race walking without people looking at you funny. Why do the Mexicans get treated different when they come to the United States? Most of them only want to work. Mexicans work for less money but still do the job without complaining. But they are still treated as if they are not human. Think about the Mexican who are famous or has money but we treat them different from other Mexican because they are a celebrity. Because of your riches or being famous the people in this world would look over your race. Stop and think about how the women are being rape every day. The women are so scared to say anything or report it. Some of the women probably wish to be dead or find a way to escape the life style. Some are judge on the behavior of another person who is the sit me race as them. We the people in the United States and the other countries need to stop judging people the same. If it wasn't for a person or Mexican teacher we probably wouldn't be able to speak Spanish. The world wouldn't have different race speaking different nor should I say 3 languages.

What about the Muslim who comes to America to open up business. Just about every corner store is own by a Muslim. Think about the motels you stay in. They are own by a different race then you are. We as Americans still go to these stores spend American money. I feel find when I go to the corner store and be treated as a regular person. Teaching the new born about Racism only cost it to continue on and keep the world from growing.

What I mean about growing is not the population. But education, jobs, and most of all sharing love that you would give to your own race. What if you or anybody was put in a life or death situation were the only person who can save you is a different race than you. What would you do? Me personally I would except that help. That how we all should look at life. It all starts at home when it comes to the kids. If your child see that you get alone with different race. The child would grow up feeling and looking at life different than someone who's older than them. I'm not saying forget about the past but stop teaching it. Some kids may learn about but at the same time see some of it's as hate. Then that child has hate in them for another race about something that went on in the past. Some of us have never experience what our elders have. So let's stop using that as a reason to hate our new breed.

You have old people and young ones who can't get Medicaid attention cause of their income. That's telling a person who in pain that there's no help for them if they don't have money. The patient with finance benefit gets help first. Is that fair to the person who was there first. There are people who needs to see a doctor but refuse to go because less income. There are people who have died but still owe money.

Some religious people may even use money in such ways of racisms. What about the money put into all these big churches. You got churches worth's millions of dollars. Okay what about the Jehovah's Witness who have a place they call a Kingdom Hall. The building is about the size of a house. This is the place where they worship god. What is the big different between the religions if they're both are praying and serving the same God. Why should a preacher get paid for preaching god news and words? If you are serving God it should be priceless. Do you see the different in how money means so much to everyone? Back in the day's religion was not back belief not for money or anyone getting paid. To me religion was something you could join without money. Look around there's a church on every corner and bigger than most schools these days. Now you see where money being spent on.